GREEDY LITTLE MARNIE AND HER WEIRD SMELLY BAG

by
Marika Rea

Mrs Appleberry Press

Copyright © 2025 Marika Rea
All rights reserved.
No part of this publication may be reproduced, stored in a retrieval system, or transmitted in any form or by any means- electronic, mechanical, photocopying, recording, or otherwise- without the prior written permission of the publisher, except in the case of brief quotations used in reviews or articles.
First edition, 2025
Illustrations by Author- assisted by AI.

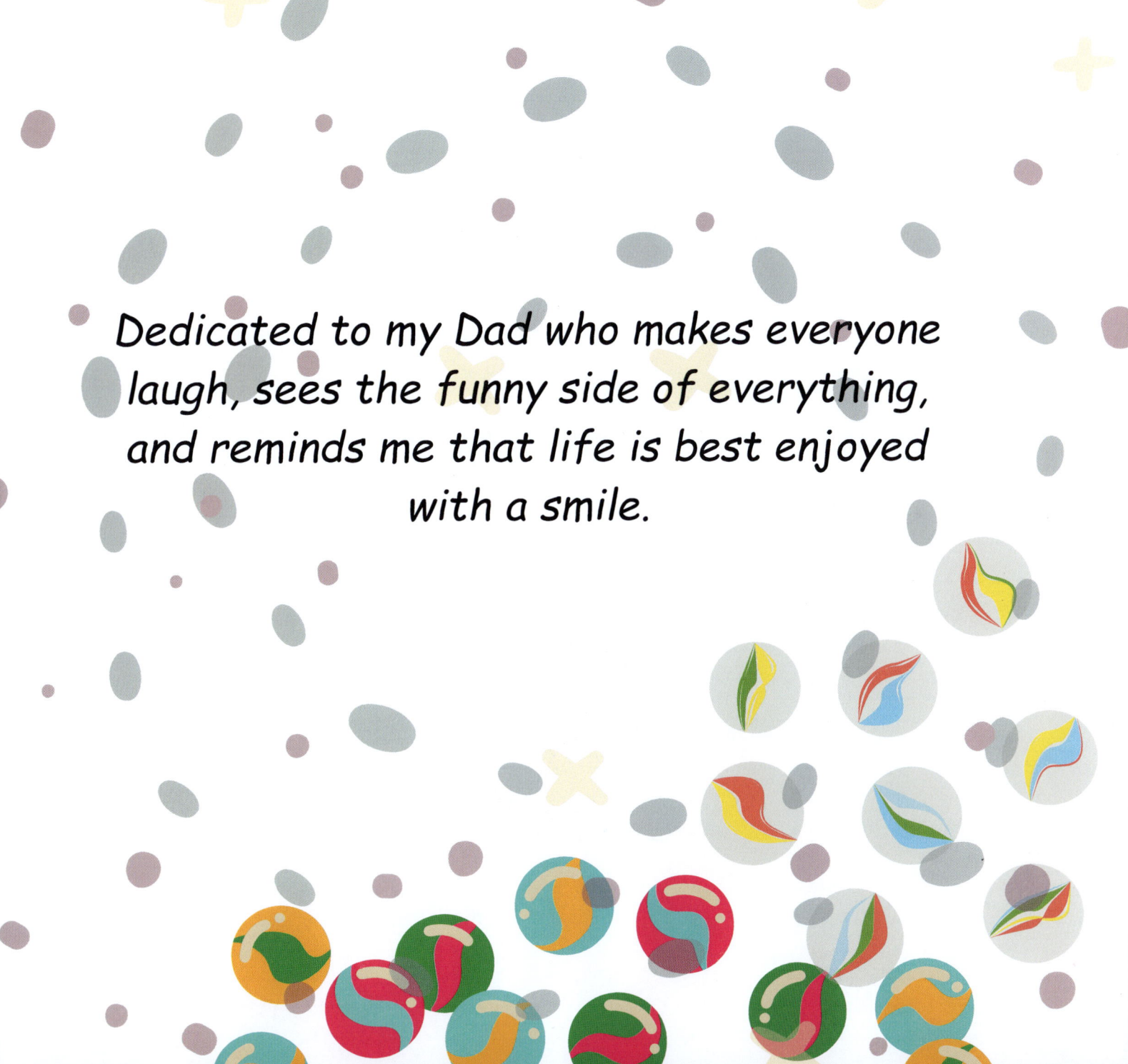

Dedicated to my Dad who makes everyone laugh, sees the funny side of everything, and reminds me that life is best enjoyed with a smile.

Author Note

Thank you for opening this little book and stepping into Marnie's world. She's a girl with a bag full of secrets, a heart full of curiosity, and a knack for finding magic in the smallest, most unexpected places.

I wrote this story to celebrate the joy of imagination, the courage of being yourself, and the little adventures that make life sparkle. Marnie's bag is strange and lumpy, but it reminds us that the most ordinary things can hold extraordinary surprises- just like us.

I hope you enjoy following Marnie on her adventures, and maybe, just maybe, you'll find a bit of your own magic along the way.

With warmth and mischief,

Marika

Marnie had a bag. Not a pretty bag. A weird bag. It was lumpy, bumpy and a bit smelly and a '*What's in there kinda bag.*' And Marnie never, ever let it go.

At school, the other kids whispered, '*What's in there*?' Some thought it was a bunch of snacks. Others thought it was homework or maybe even a puppy.

When nobody was looking - Marnie would climb inside. Down she tumbled, through strings of fairy lights, past shelves of spinning teapots and over a bridge made of biscuit crumbs.

This was 'Bag World' and Bag World was enormous.

There was the Mayor's silver spoon (good for stirring chocolate lakes.)

And there was Old Mrs. O'Grady's green umbrella (now a flying boat.)

In Bag World, Marnie could be anything - a pirate with a crown, or a queen with a cat army.

A detective with a cape made from stolen picnic blankets.

Before she could run, a tide of marbles swept her away.

Her cheeks burned hot. *'I'm sorry,'* she whispered. Bag World sighed... and began to shrink.

She climbed out of her bag, arms aching from carrying so much stuff back from Bag World.

But now it was mostly filled with drawings, bicuits she baked herself and tiny gifts she asked for.

Thanks for reading

If you enjoyed this book, please leave a review on Amazon and help other kids discover this story.

Other titles by Marika Rea:

Now on Amazon. Check out my website www.mrsappleberrypress.ie for more details.

Children's Books

Fiorella Can't Jump
What I Know For Certain
The Boy Who Followed Me
Taka the Wolf
The Girl Whose Hair Wouldn't Grow

Printed in Dunstable, United Kingdom